BY NATHAN LUMM

I was going through some backup files and came across an old flier for an art show. This one was for my second solo show, "The Rest Of Us". The main theme of the show was to depict normal everyday people and to show that we are all the same. We're all in this together and all that. I had a nice write up in the local weekly newspaper about the show. There was even a comparison of my art to the likes of Dan Clowes and his work on Ghost World. I didn't see it, but I'll take the compliment. I remember that night being full of disappointment. I was working on this show for months. I was putting in the hours after work and on the weekends and really trying to say something with this show. I think a grand total of 4 people came by for the opening. Two of which were a co-worker and her husband. I think Mark Mothersbaugh, of Devo fame, had an opening that same night at another gallery. But, yeah, I was pretty gutted.

My first solo show was titled "Beneath the Depths" and featured more cartoony style paintings of fish and various sea life. I liked those paintings well enough, but there was no purpose, no statement. It just was. And people showed up for it. A couple paintings even sold. I was happy and all, I just wished there was more to it. So that's what I tried to do with "The Rest of Us". And nobody gave a shit.

I still wonder to this day why that show was such a failure. I mean as far as turnout. I wasn't concerned about the money or if anything sold, I was doing pretty well at my job at the time. Was the timing off? Keep in mind this show was over 10 years ago now, back in 2009. We were just seeing the 2008 "Financial Crisis" and the implications of what it might mean for the future. Maybe it was too ahead of it's time and everyone was still trying to pretend that they weren't being affected by it. This was in Fort Lauderdale after all. I used to think Los Angeles was full of fake people. But Southern Florida has them beat hands down. Maybe it was just the wrong place for this show. Sure, there are some bad parts of Fort Lauderdale, every place has them, but there are also million dollar mansions, yachts, up-scale hotels and pricey bars. What the hell do they care about the people that are having a harder time than them? Maybe it would have been a better idea to add biographies underneath the paintings at the show, instead of relying on the viewers to make up their own stories.

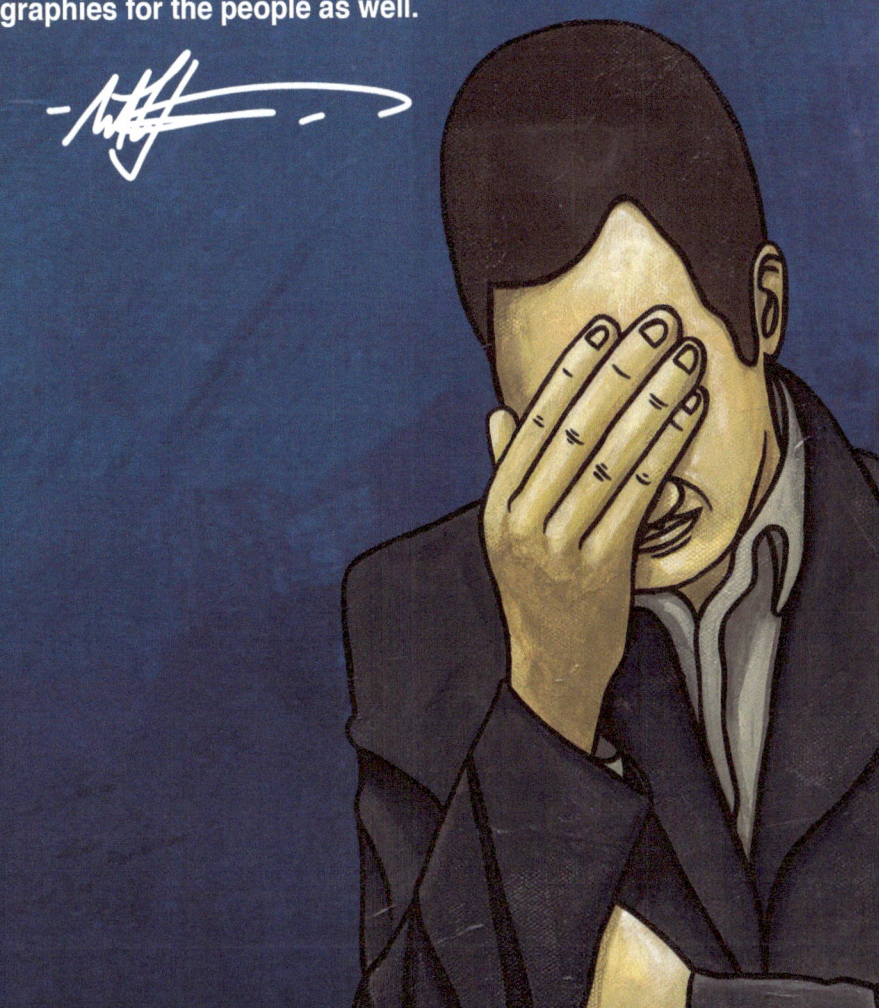

But let's be real. I wasn't living check to check. I certainly wasn't rich, but I was able to take care of the bills and have money left over. I had some hard times earlier in my life, and harder times now, but I wasn't there, at that spot, when I was working on these paintings. Maybe I wasn't putting everything I had into them. Or maybe people just saw them as random portraits and didn't care to read into anything more than that.

I don't know. I'll never know. Maybe one day I'll come to terms with that. One thing I do know is that I still believe in this series.

For this retrospective, I've collected the 14 paintings along with some pictures from the opening night. I also found some old drawings that didn't make the cut for this show, so those are included as well. Lastly, I went ahead and added some biographies for the people as well.

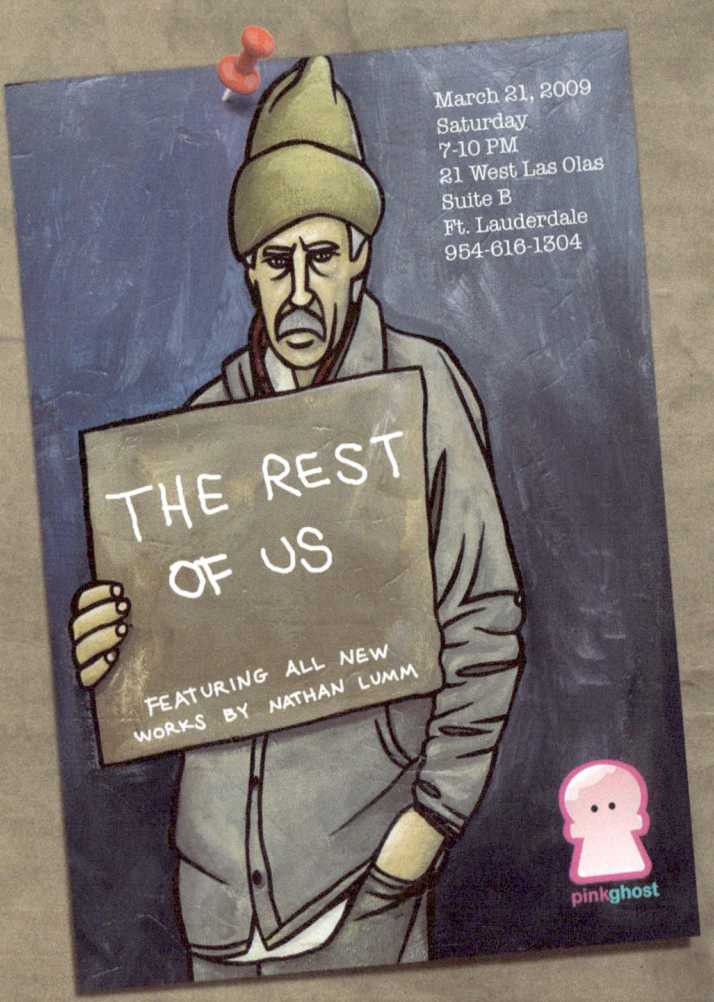

FLYER

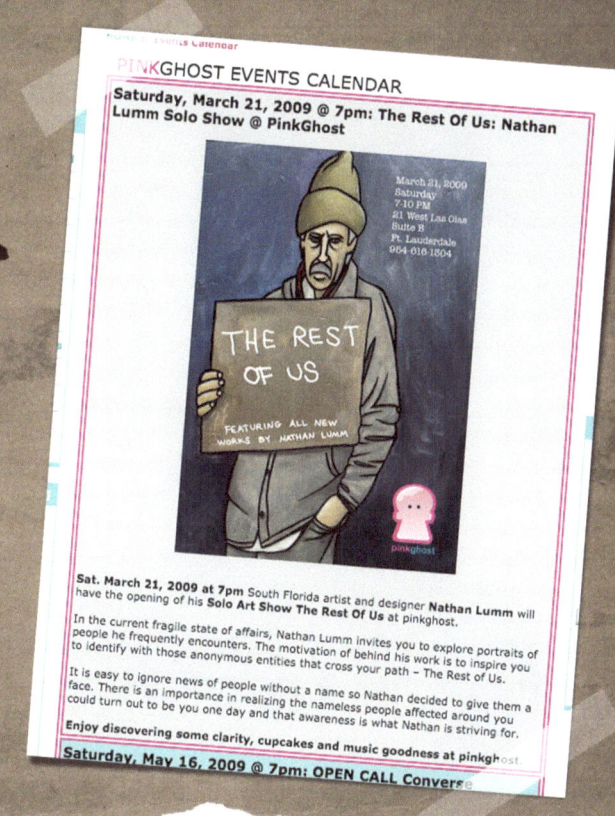

PINKGHOST EVENTS CALENDAR

Saturday, March 21, 2009 @ 7pm: The Rest Of Us: Nathan Lumm Solo Show @ PinkGhost

March 21, 2009
Saturday
7-10 PM
81 West Las Olas
Suite B
Ft. Lauderdale
954-616-1804

THE REST OF US

FEATURING ALL NEW WORKS BY NATHAN LUMM

pinkghost

Sat. March 21, 2009 at 7pm South Florida artist and designer **Nathan Lumm** will have the opening of his **Solo Art Show The Rest Of Us** at pinkghost.

In the current fragile state of affairs, Nathan Lumm invites you to explore portraits of people he frequently encounters. The motivation of behind his work is to inspire you to identify with those anonymous entities that cross your path – The Rest of Us.

It is easy to ignore news of people without a name so Nathan decided to give them a face. There is an importance in realizing the nameless people affected around you could turn out to be you one day and that awareness is what Nathan is striving for.

Enjoy discovering some clarity, cupcakes and music goodness at pinkghost.

Saturday, May 16, 2009 @ 7pm: OPEN CALL Converse

In times of hardship and recession, it's easy for all of us to close our selves off from everybody else, and just worry about ourselves. In his second solo show with PinkGhost, Nathan Lumm showcases all new portraits of everyday hardworking people as a reminder to everyone that we're all in same boat. Let's not forget about the homeless guy on the corner, or the guy that works at the local fast food joint, or the lady that answers the phone when you have a problem with your ATM card. No matter how good you think you have it or how much better you think you are than everybody else, it can all be swept away in an instant and you'll be down here with the rest of us.

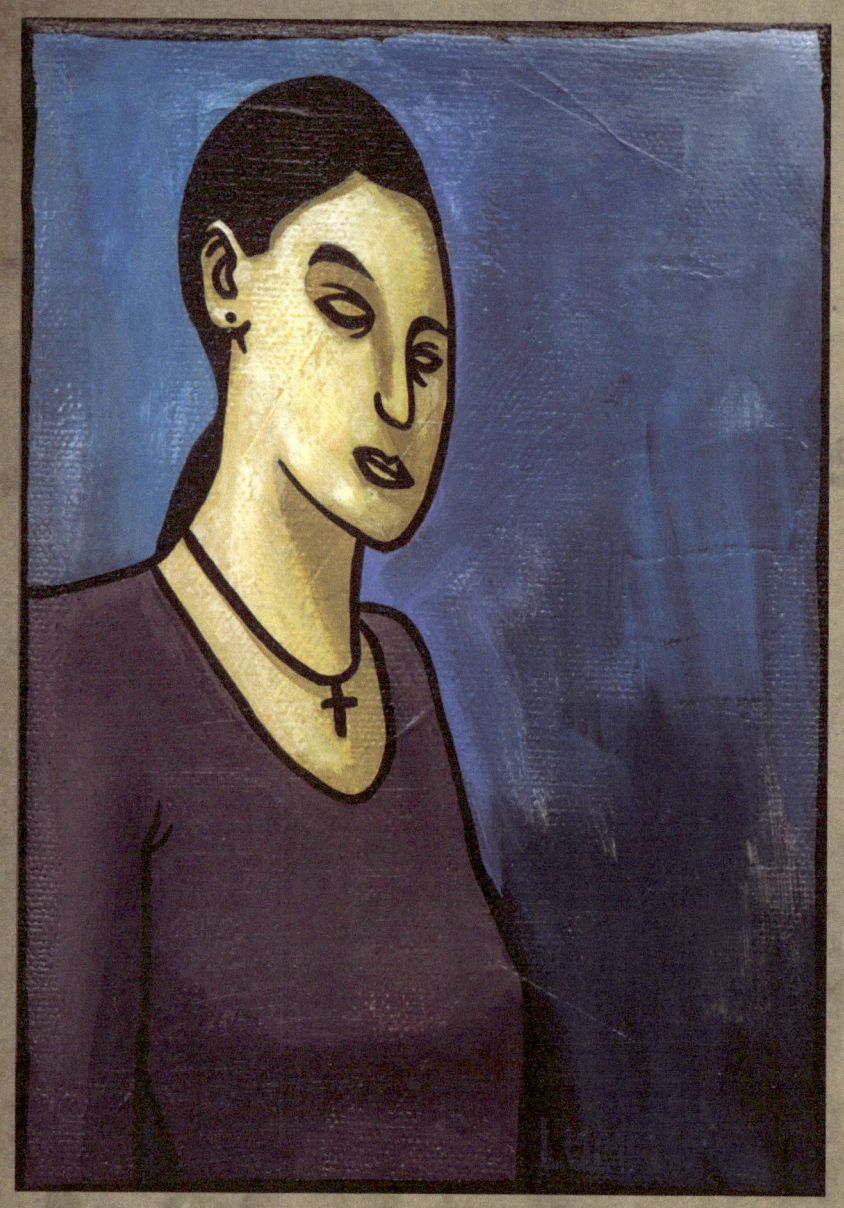

This is Mary. She is a server at a popular lunch spot downtown. She gets no health benefits and has to depend on people not to be shitty and tip properly so she can cover her bills.

Tom was just laid off from his job that he held for 32 years. He gave his heart and soul to the company and has no transferrable skills to show for it. At the age of 50, he is now starting at the bottom of the ladder at a new company.

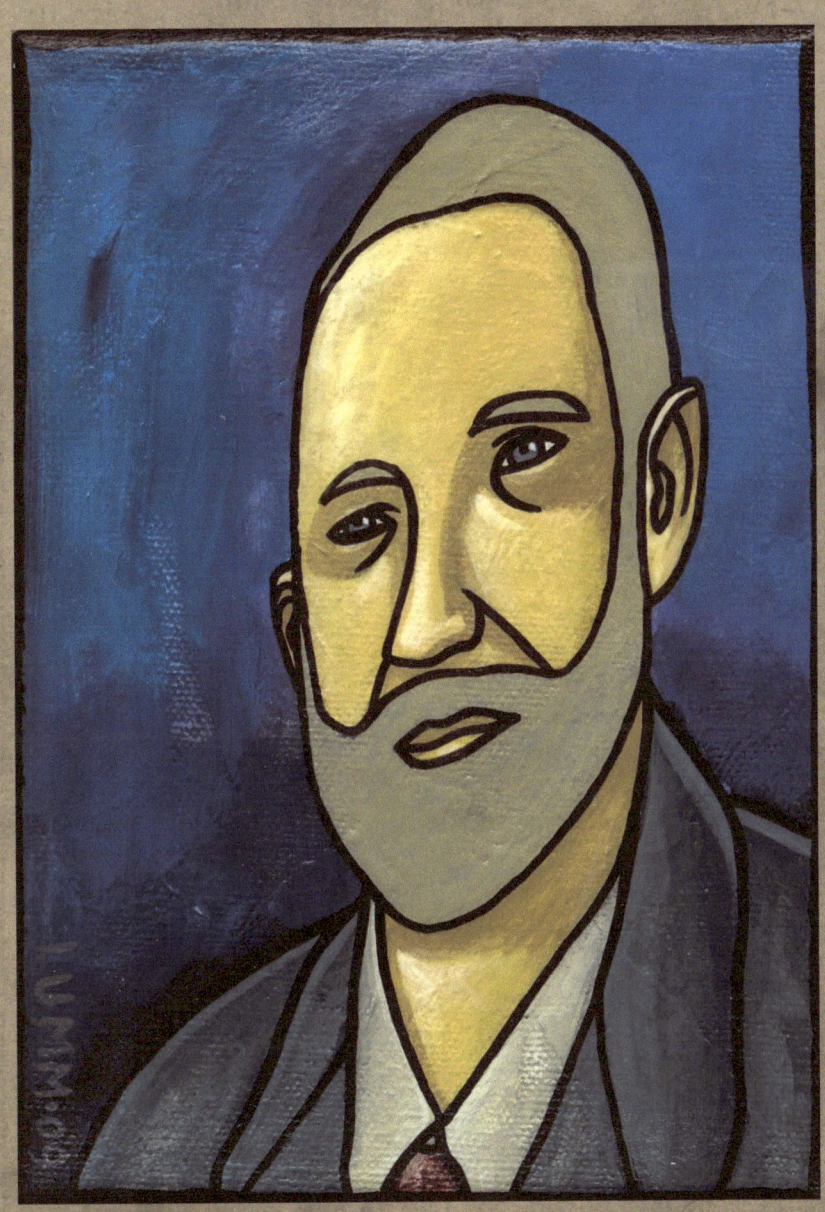

Richard, here, works in sales. He hates his job, and is forced to be dishonest with his clients in order to keep his sales numbers up. Another bad month, and he'll be let go.

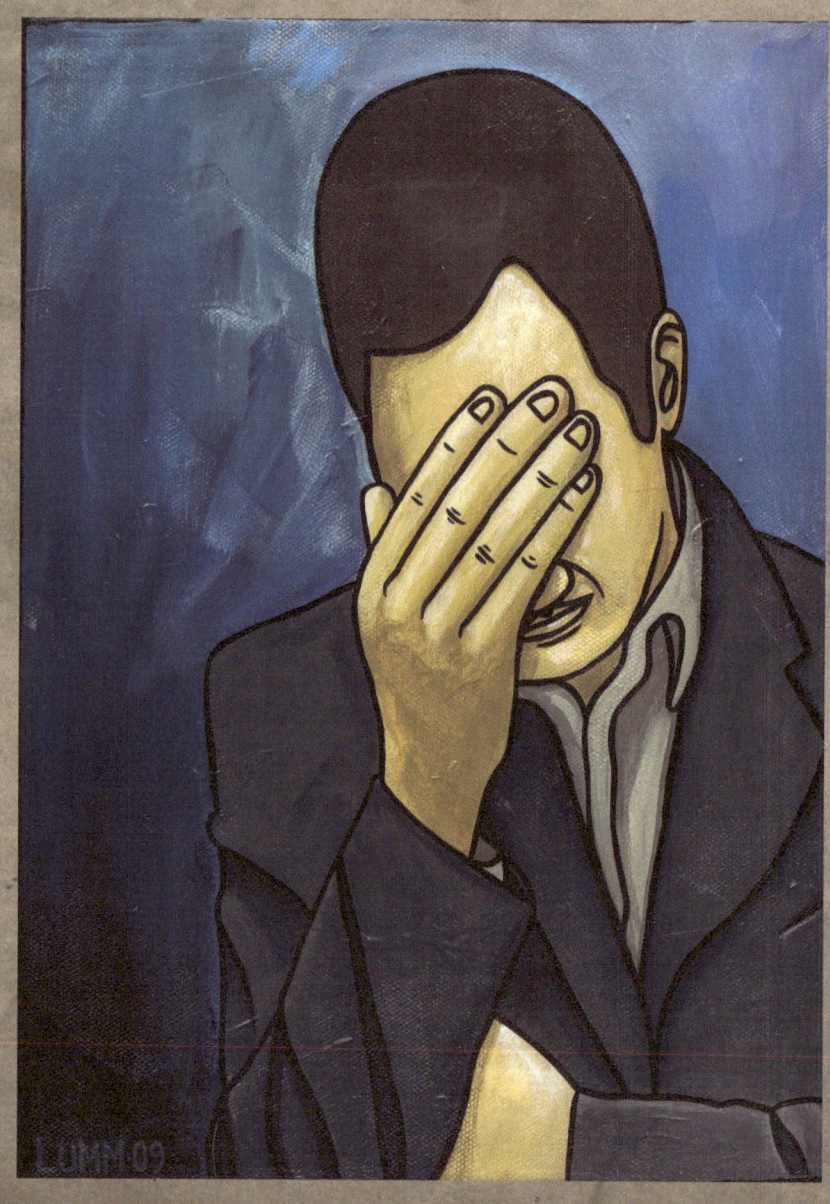

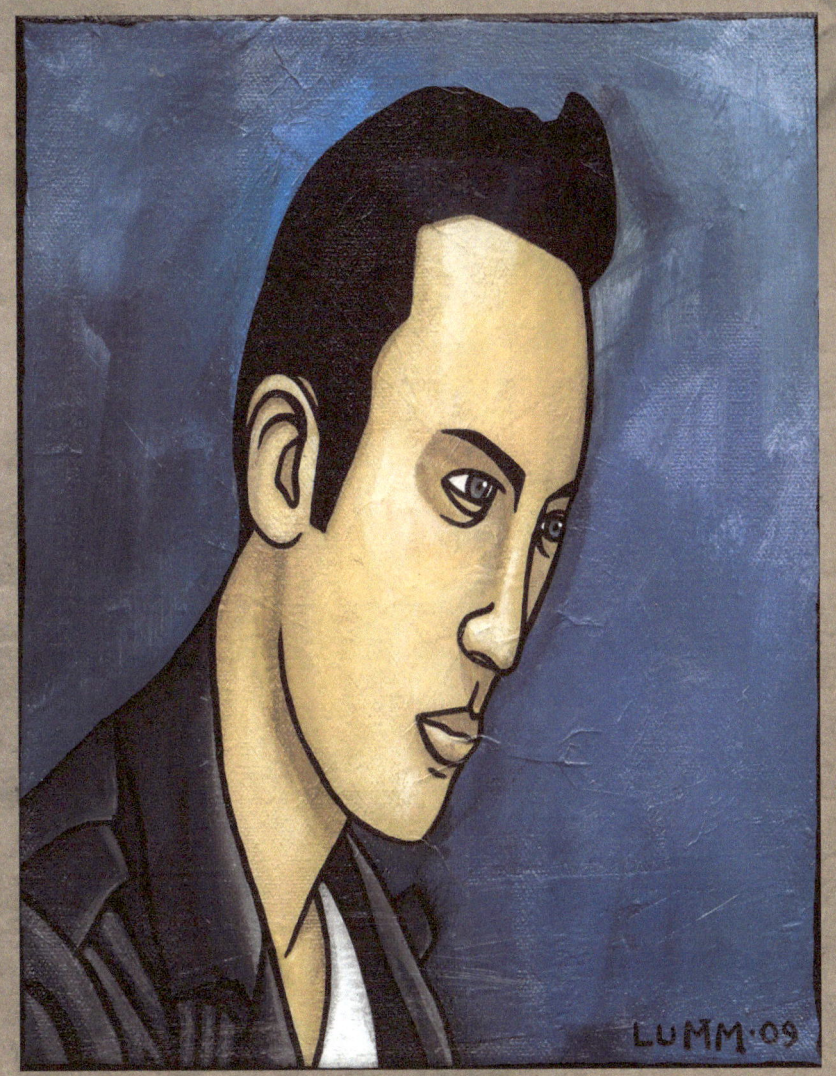

LUMM·09

Jack works two jobs just to keep the lights on. Sure, he might be able to find a cheaper place to live, but then his daughter would have to move to a worse school. He used to be in a band, but had to give it up right before the record deal, in order to make money.

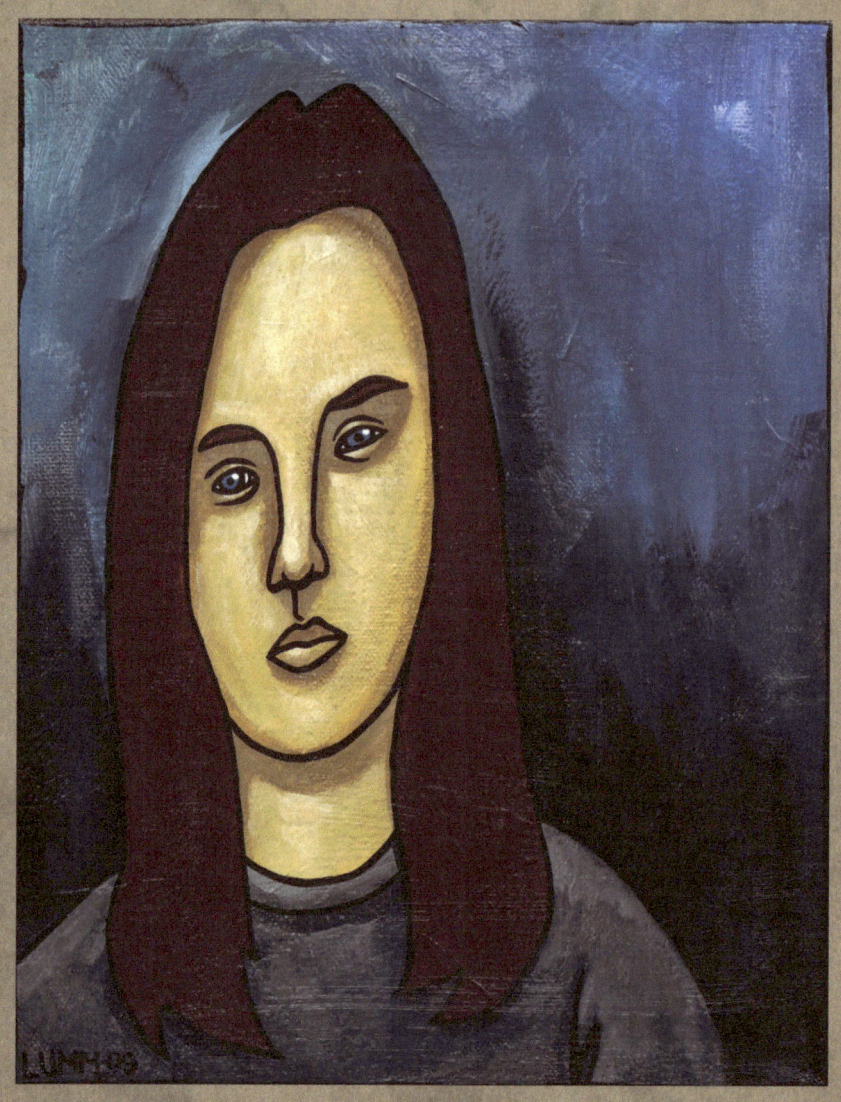

Shelly is a struggling artist trying to find her big break. She attends the local openings and tries to get noticed by the gallery owners, but she refuses to kiss anybody's ass.

James is an old soul. Not much is known about him. He shows up on random nights at the local hole-in-the-wall bar and everybody know him. Also, he can sing the hell out of the blues on karaoke night.

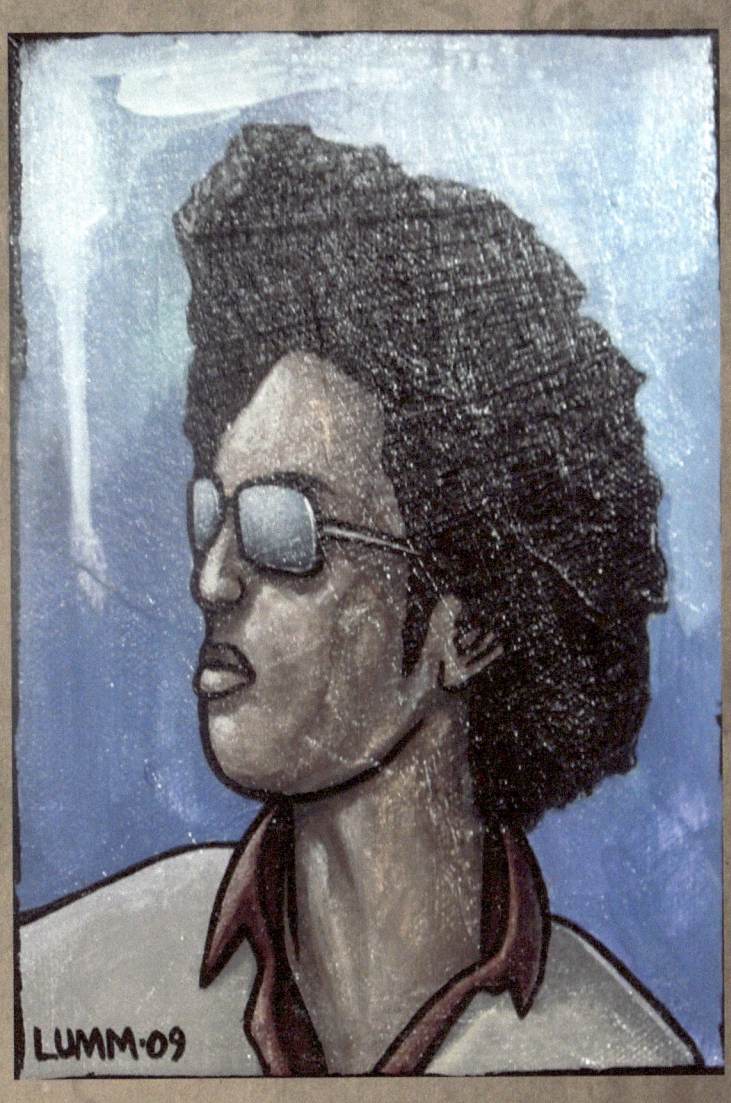

OPENING NIGHT!

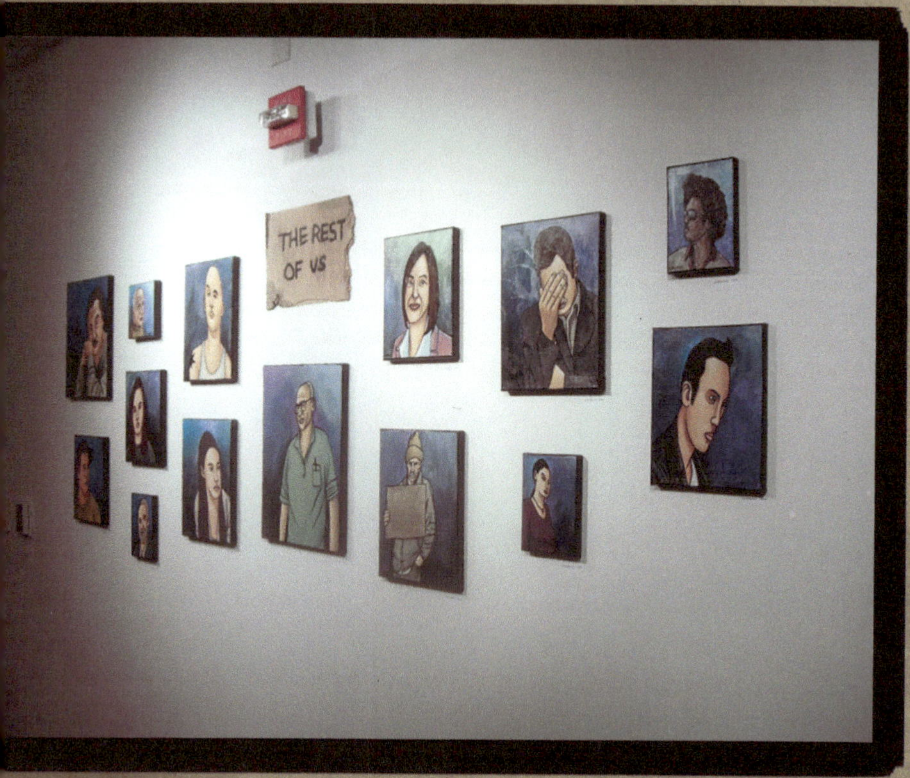

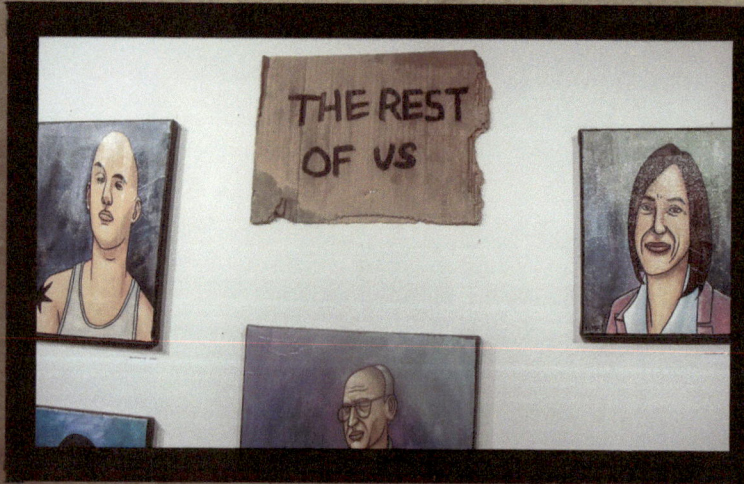

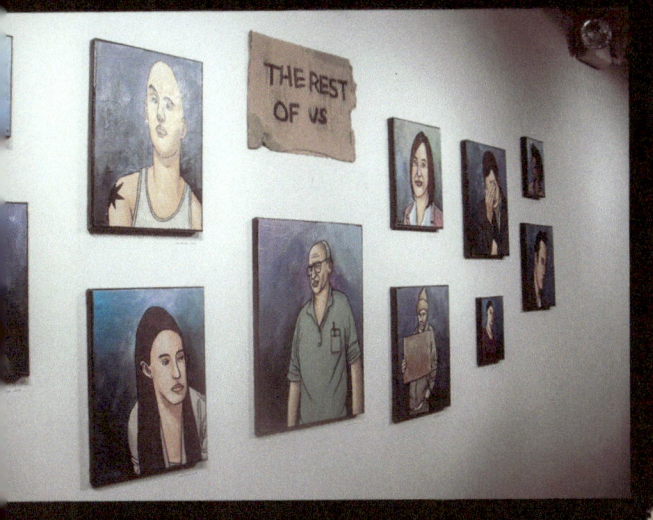

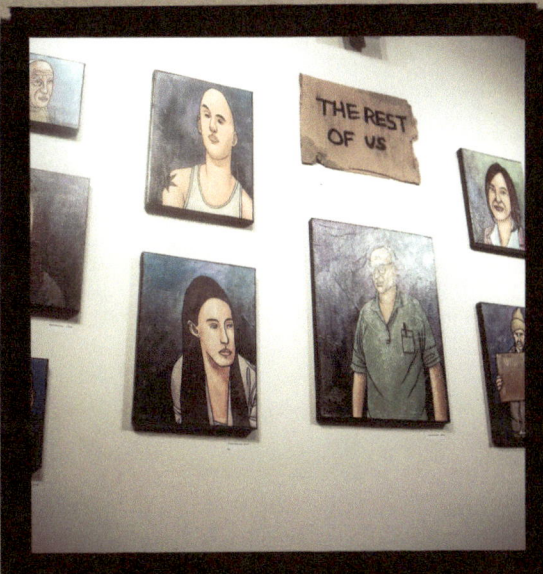

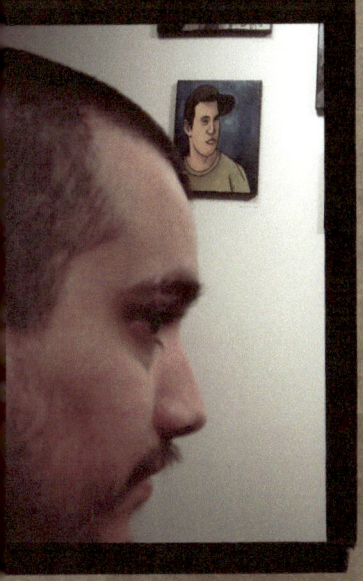

MY
DISAPPOINTED
LOOK

Robert works in the kitchen at a steakhouse. He has a drug habit that he claims he has under control. If he gets fired from this job, it will be his fourth in six months.

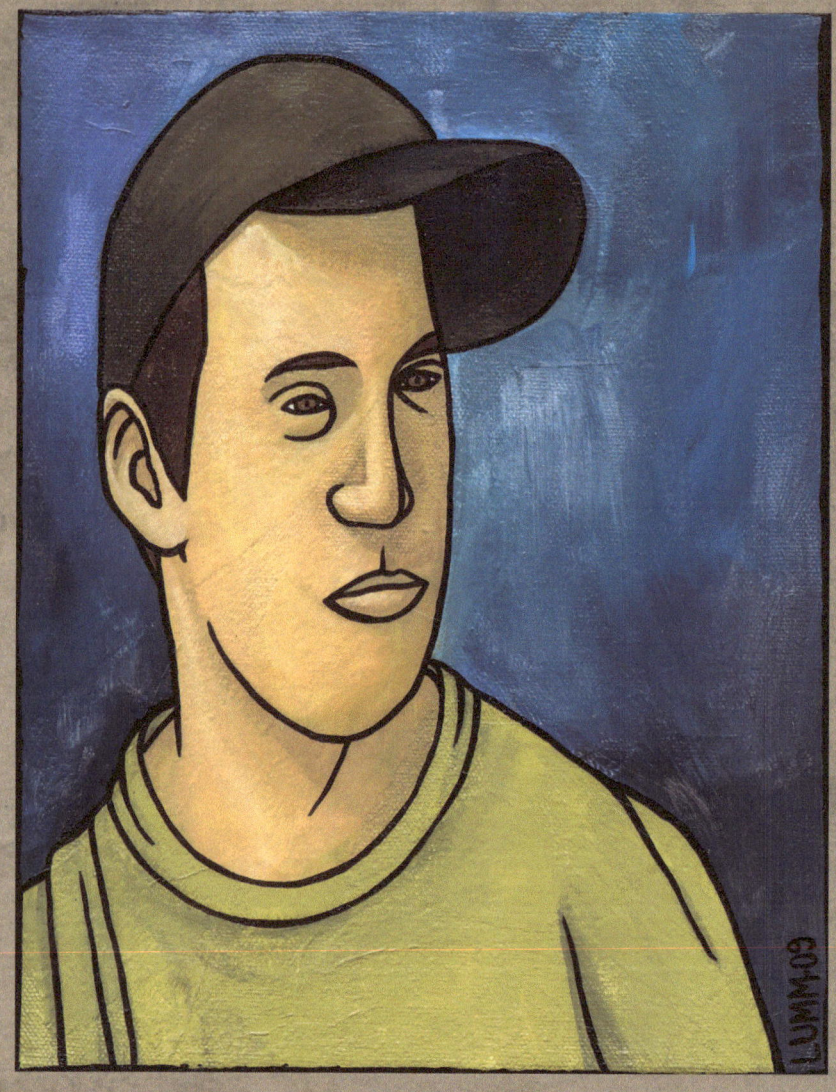

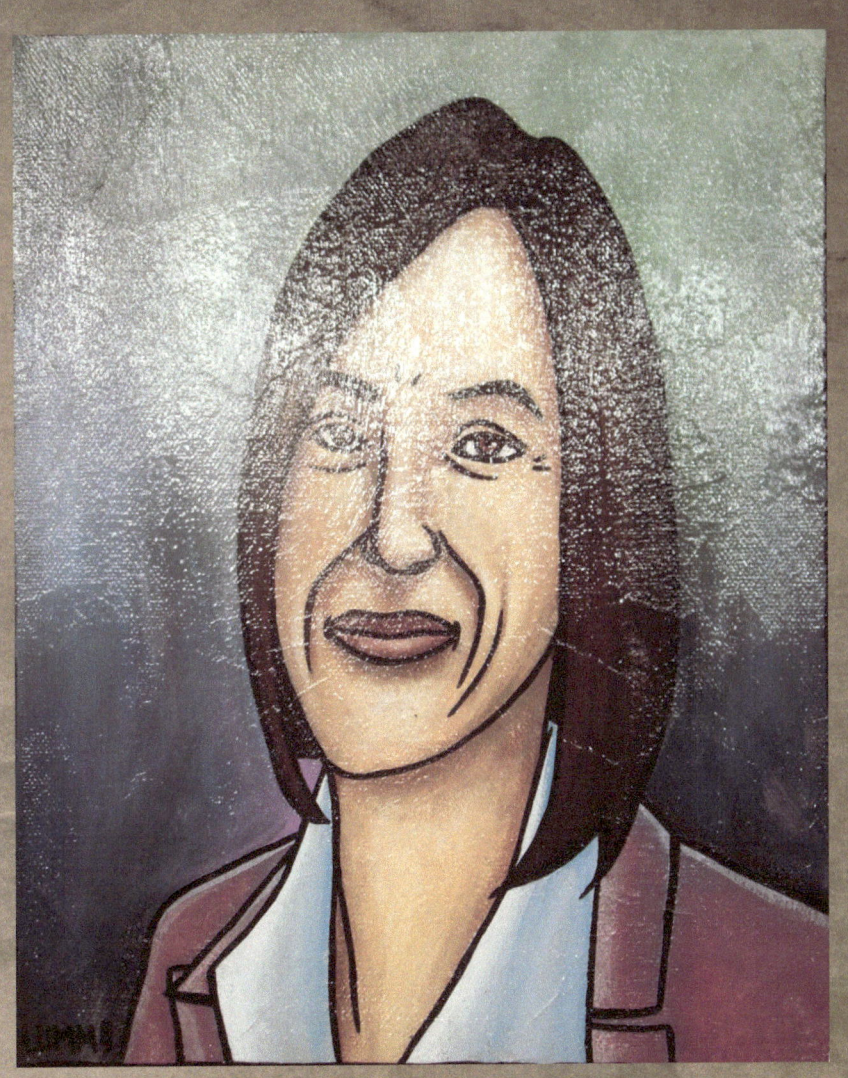

This is Karen. She is an account manager at a bank. Currently, her manager is blaming her for somebody else's shoddy work. She needs this job to pay for a lawyer for her teenage son, who just got arrested for shoplifting.

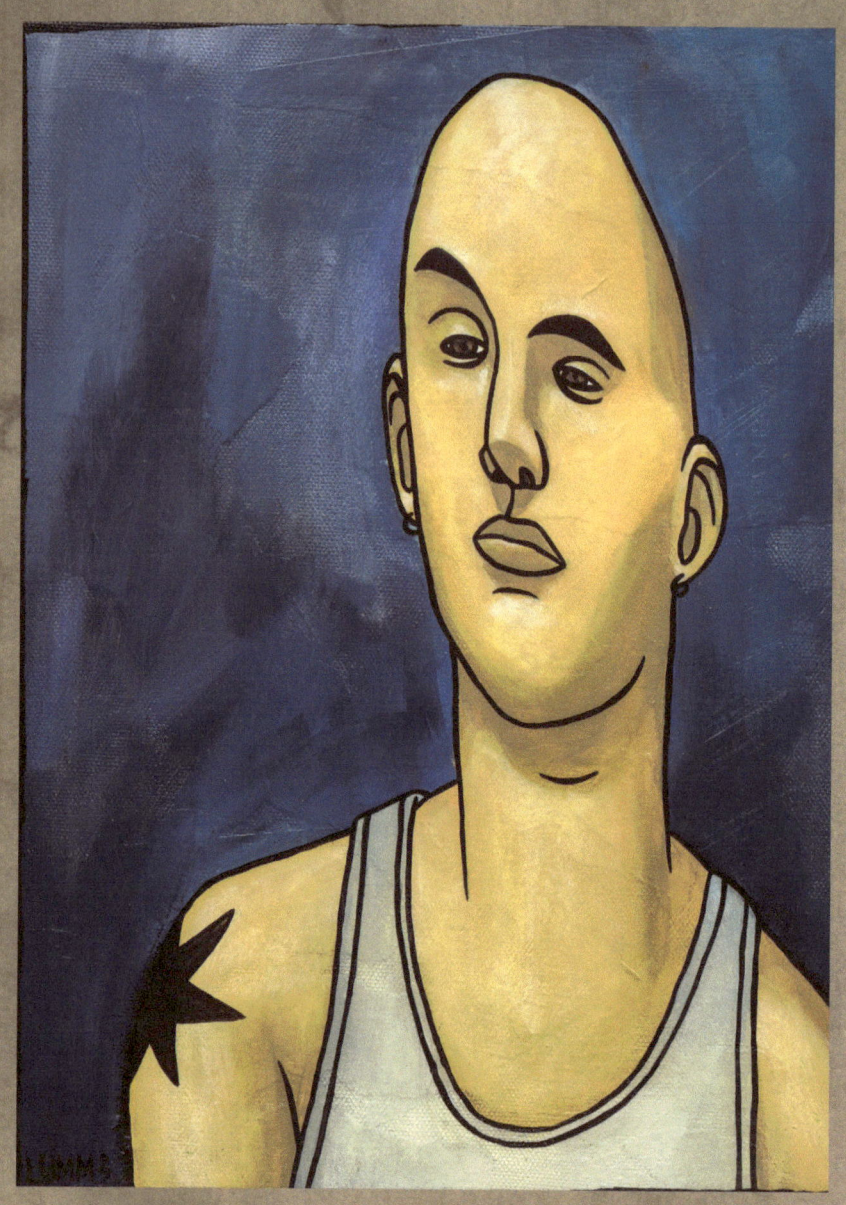

Mikey is a bouncer at one of the downtown bars. He was breaking up a fight where three guys were jumping on one. His arm got busted, in the process, and has no idea how he's going to pay his hospital bill.

Edward has been planning his retirement for years. He got a call from his accountant that fills him in on the market slowing down. He'll have to postpone his retirement another five years. This is the third time he's had to postpone.

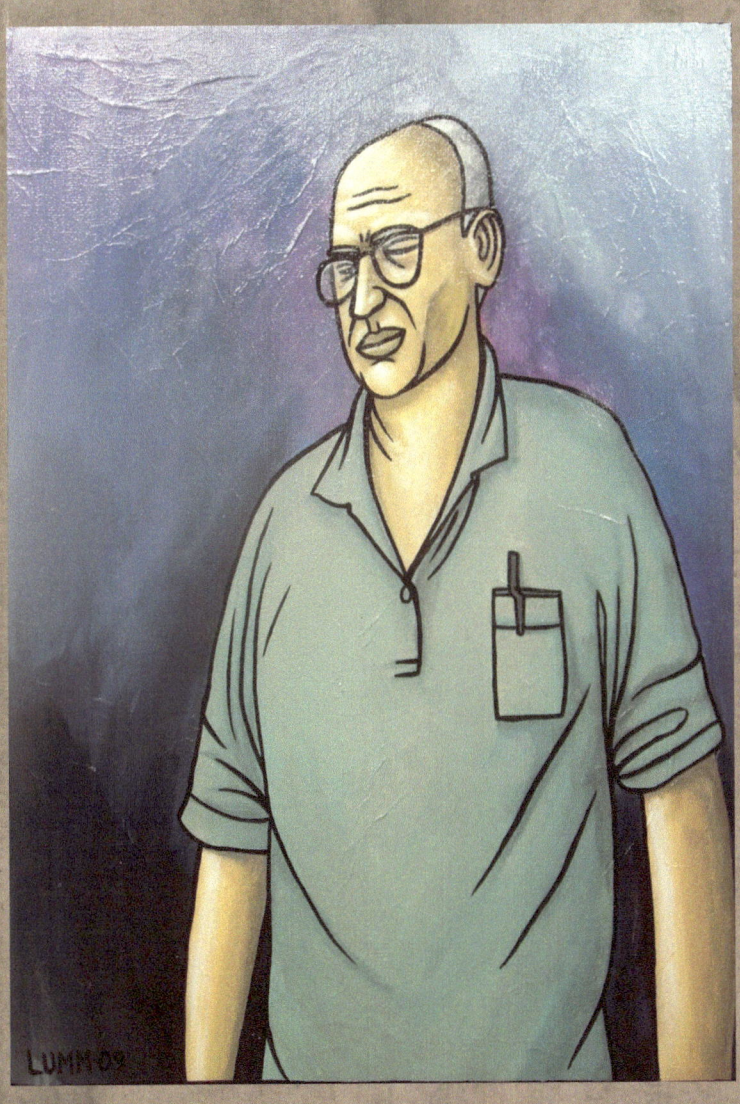

Walter was a successful lawyer until one day he was t-boned by a bus. He got addicted to pain pills, lost his job and family, and ended up on the streets. He has since cleaned himself up and is selling pamphlets of his poetry to help him get back on his feet.

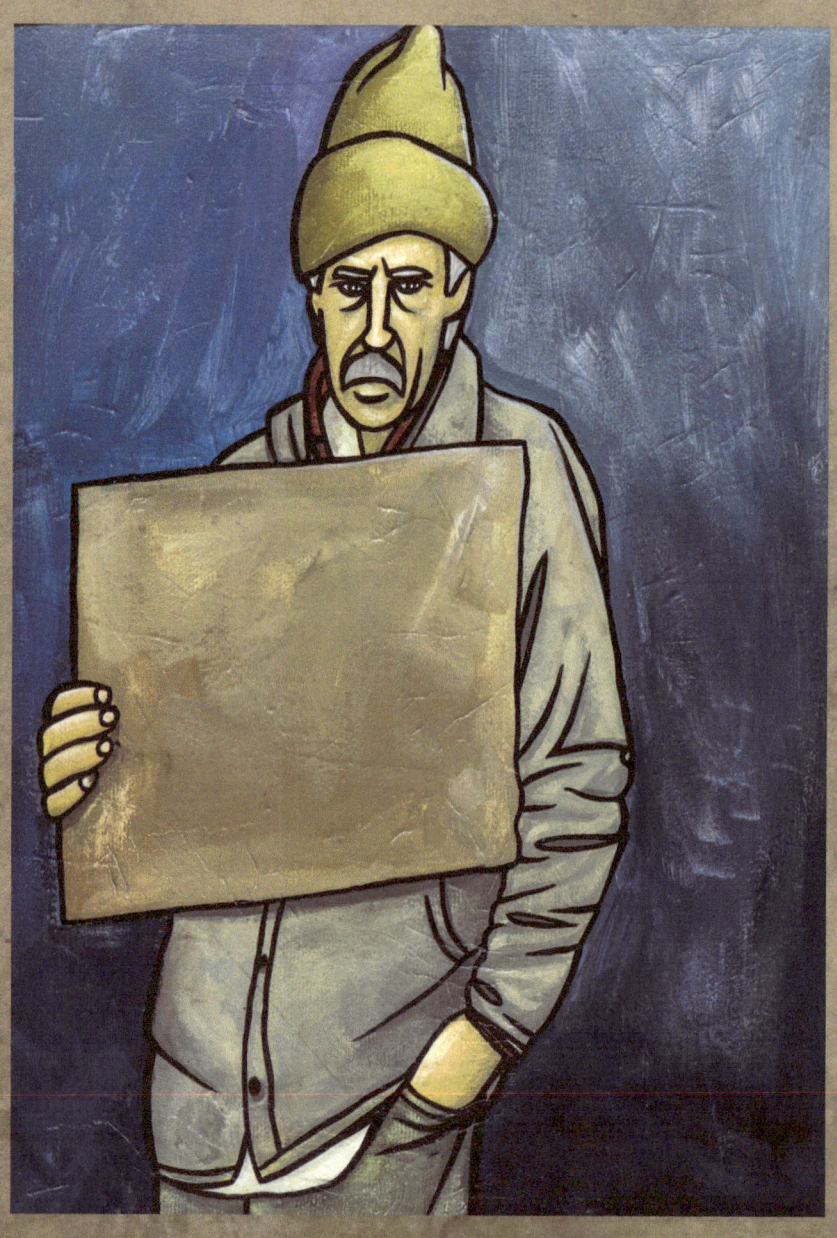

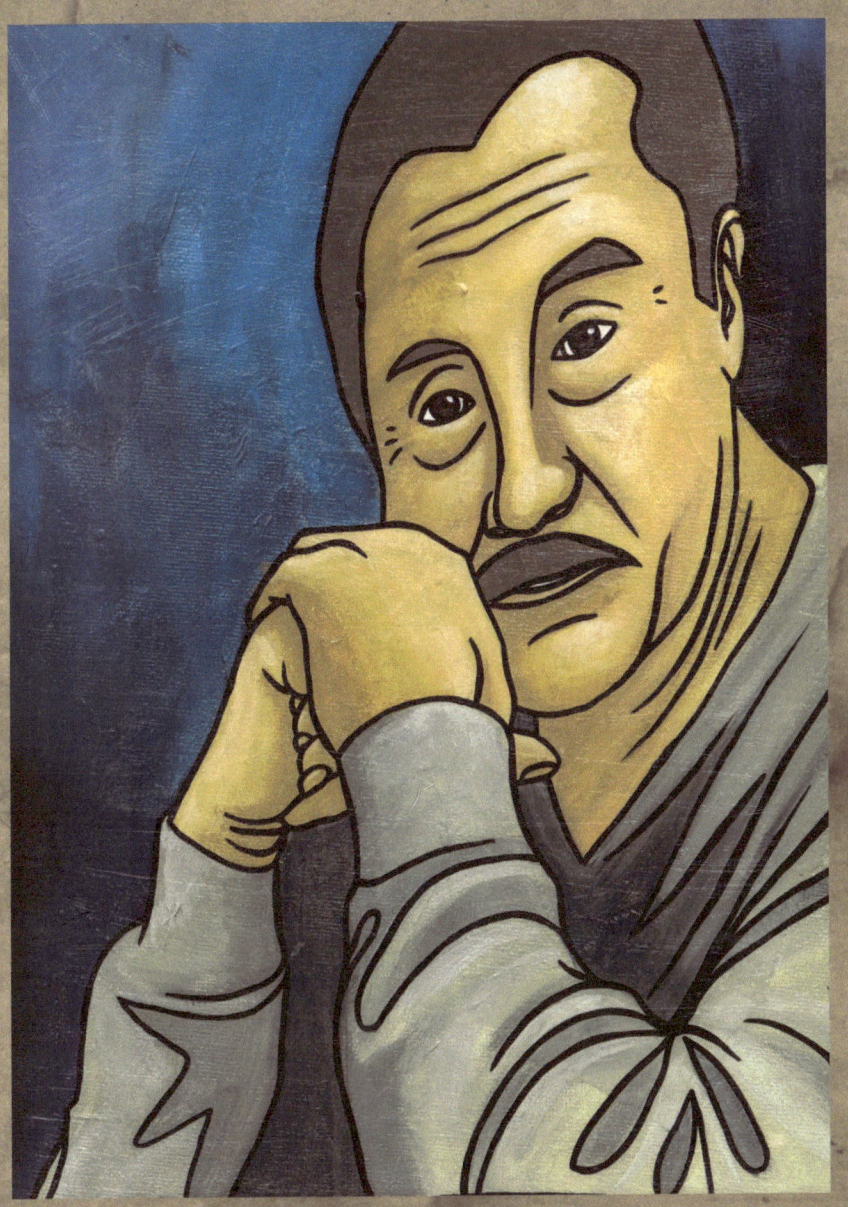

Henry works the midnight shift at the plant. He use to have a comfortable position working during the days, but had to give up that shift so he could watch his grand-kids, while his daughter was looking for work. She just moved back home after finding her husband sleeping with his co-worker.

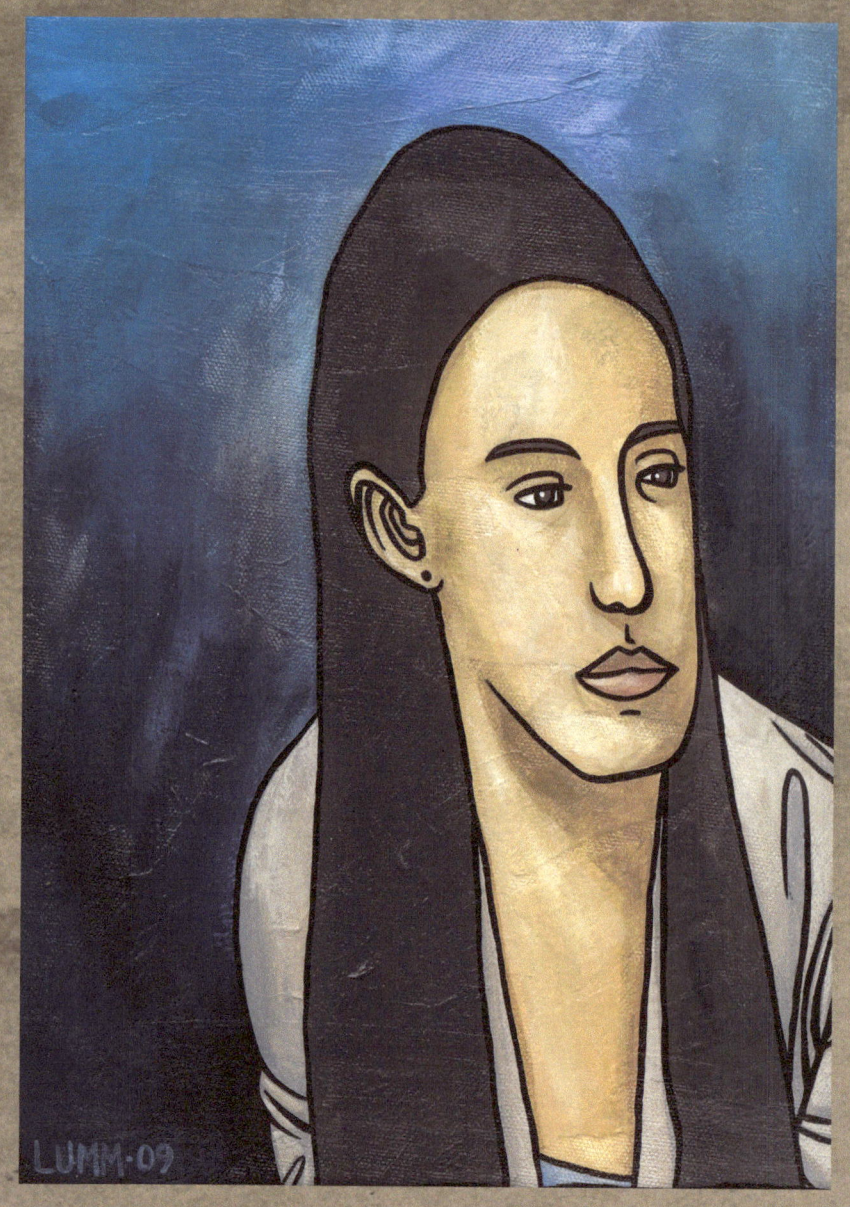

Miranda just got a letter from her landlord saying that they are raising her rent again. She can move to another place but then she would have to come up with all the moving fees, plus security deposit, and first and last months rent. Or should she just stay and put up with the increase?

Pablo owns a deli in the trendy part of town. He stays up late each night going over the books to see if they can make it till the end of the lease. He tries to keep this away from his wife so that she doesn't worry.

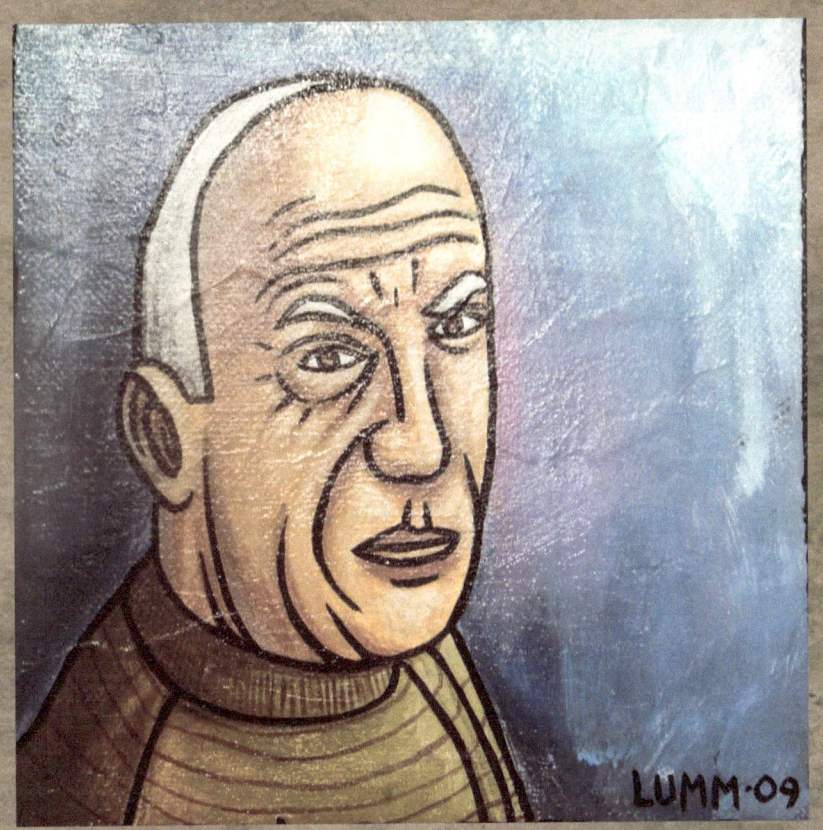

LUMM·09

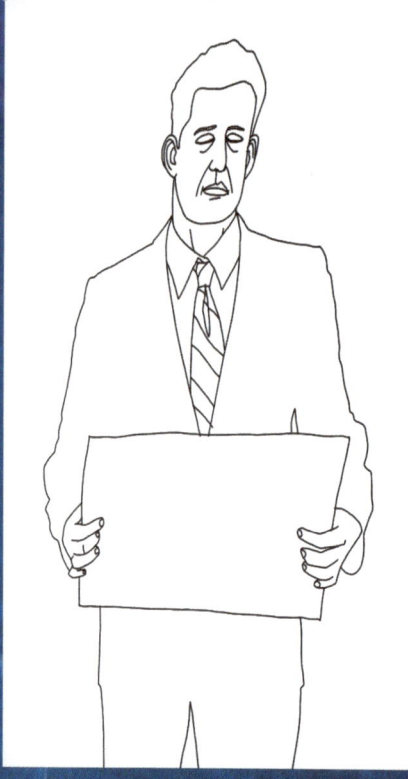

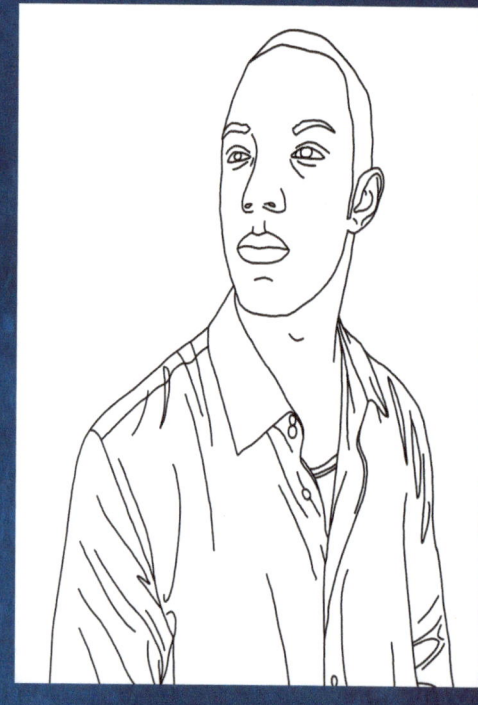

HERE ARE SOME MORE PEOPLE THAT DIDN'T QUITE MAKE THE CUT FOR ONE REASON OR ANOTHER. SOME OF THESE WERE EVENTUALLY USED FOR OTHER PAINTINGS.

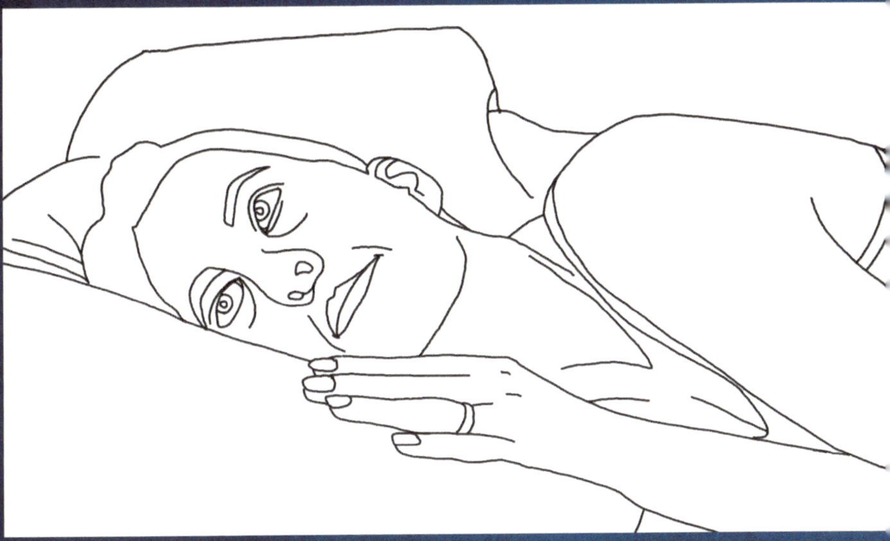

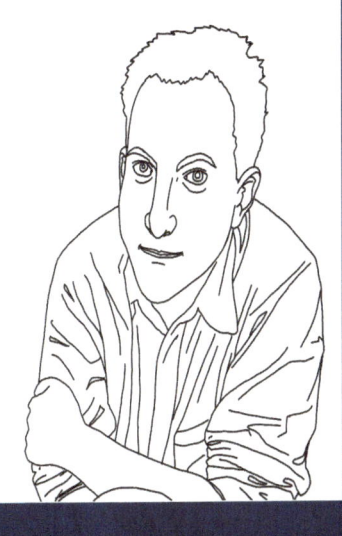
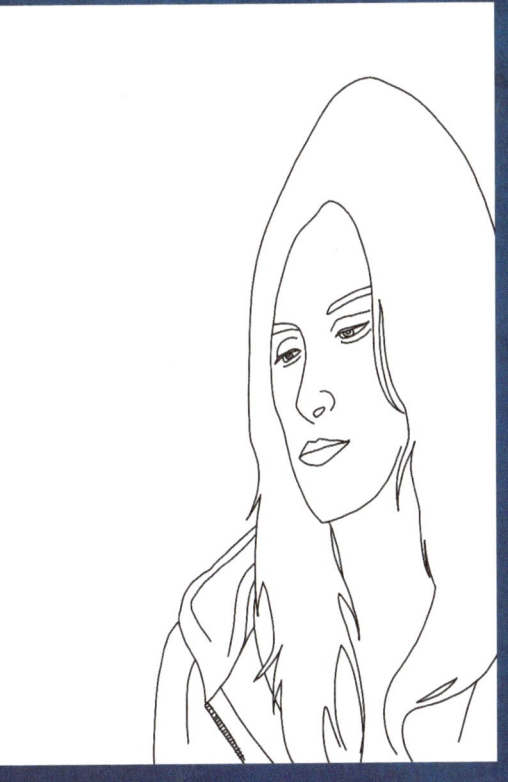

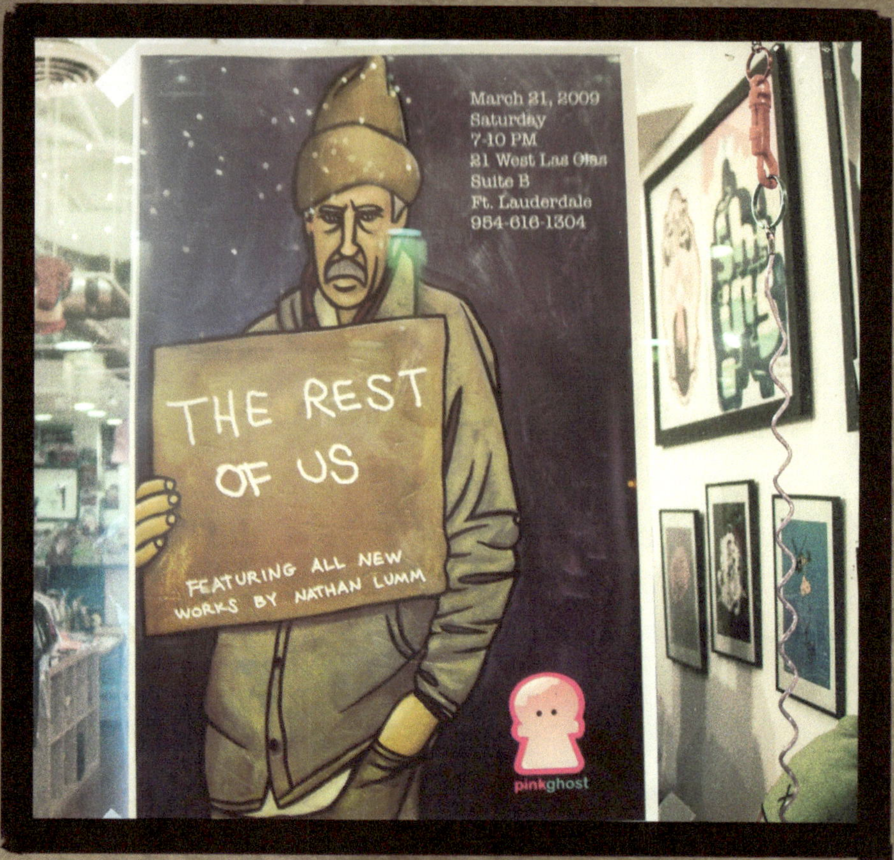

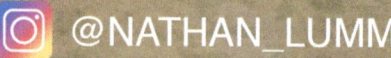

THANKS FOR ALL THE SUPPORT OVER THE YEARS!

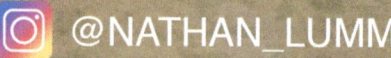 @NATHAN_LUMM

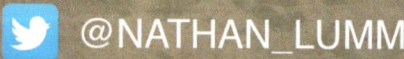 @NATHAN_LUMM

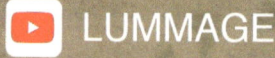 LUMMAGE

www.ingramcontent.com/pod-product-compliance
Lightning Source LLC
Chambersburg PA
CBHW041212180526
45172CB00006B/1241

* 9 7 8 1 0 8 0 8 3 2 0 6 4 *